CLASSIFICATION: POETRY

A CIP catalogue record for this book is available from the British Library.

Printed and bound in Great Britain.

Paper used in the production of books published by United Press comes only from sustainable forests.

This South East Shires (Bedfordshire, Berkshire, Buckinghamshire, Hampshire, Hertfordshire, Oxfordshire) and South West edition

ISBN 978-1-84436-565-4

First published in Great Britain in 2007 by
United Press Ltd
Admail 3735
London
EC1B 1JB
Tel: 0870 240 6190
Fax: 0870 240 6191
ISBN for complete set of volumes
978-1-84436-566-1

www.unitedpress.co.uk

Poetic Fantasy

Foreword

By its very nature every poem is a fantasy - a flight of fancy. That's because every time a poet puts pen to paper he or she creates a work of art which comes from his or her fertile imagination.

This, of course, means that people who write poetry need to possess that wonderful gift - the skill to create something which is truly fantastic - just by using their thought processes.

Within the pages of this anthology you will find that a large number of individual poets have created their own personal fantasy.

Each one is surprisingly and wonderfully different. Each one is an open door into a realm of dreams - an expression of something deeply personal - their own *Poetic Fantasy.*

I hope that you, the reader, can enjoy the fantasies, identify with them, understand them, empathise with them. Above all we hope you delight in the sheer wonder that is the human imagination - that amazing gift of nature which gives birth to poetry.

Lynda Brennan, Editor

Contents

The poets who have contributed to this volume are listed below, along with the relevant page upon which their work can be found.

62 Sandra Whelan
63 Elaina Swiffen
64 Sally-Ann Deakin
65 Barbara Featherstone
Jean Gillmore
66 Lisa Combellack
67 Vicki Terry-Short
Philip Davey
68 Alan Hayden
69 Edna S J Williams
70 Margaret Beaumont
71 Jason Dawes
Malcolm Swingler
72 Phil Goldman
73 Gillie Morris
74 Frank Beer
75 Susie Burns
Stella Redman
76 Derrick Roach
77 Cha Cha Farrow
78 Rian Mikalauskas
Yvonne Streeter
79 Sophia Eve Roddan
80 Roslyn C Baxter
81 Lorraine Shaw
82 Gemma Thomson
Harry Webb
83 Helen Gallagher
84 Michael Woodhouse
Sheila Evans
85 Audrey Pope
86 Tracy Leadbeater
Patricia Stuckey
87 Janis Naylor
88 Sammy Davis
Betty Aldworth
89 Wendy Smith
90 Margaret Willis
Susan Emptage
91 Reg Rowe
92 Janet Huck
93 Albert Lewis
Joan Fricker
94 David Johnson
Andrew Gissing
95 Eileen Prewett
96 Vincent Oakes
Keith Howard
97 Wendy Day
Shirley Clift
98 John Anthony
99 Glenn Mower
100 Stella Lamb
Maryrose Ferrier
101 Raymond Pearce
Judy Robinson
102 Giles Highnam
103 Charlotte Edmonds
Gillian Layzell
104 Violetta Ferguson
105 Melanie Jones
Maurice Carpenter
106 Caroline Vennard
107 Pamela J Hacking
108 Nicola Woodley
Michael Elliott
109 Margaret Cawsey
110 Florence L Brain
111 Joan Lake
Sam Davis
112 Lynsey Wootton
113 Patricia Shellis
Jacqui Shipway
114 Douglas Hoyle
115 Colin Threader
116 Maurice W Fawcett
Bee K Watson
117 Alex Date
118 Pam Jewell
119 Colin Mann
Betty Bywater
120 Joan Rowland
121 Percy J Harrison
Barbara M Crisp
122 Patrick Jefferies
123 Marc Richards

Margaret R Punter
124 Angela James
125 Valerie Hembry
Helen Guymer
126 Patrick Hutchinson
127 Dorothy S Keene
Clive Blake
128 Paul Fancett
129 Barry Ryan

THE WILD GARDEN

It's totally wild - out of control,
haven for hedgehog, mouse or vole.

But come out rodents, if you dare;
the vixen's stirring in her lair.

Dark trees are looming up above.
Do I feel a hand, giving me a shove?

Eerie sounds, I hear this night,
would give the bravest soul a fright.

A cat, as black as coal glides by,
only visible by her glinting eye.

And on this ink-black, starry night;
I sense the swish of broomstick's flight.

That cackling witch is on the prowl,
alerted by a hooting owl.

Large bats are circling overhead;
I'm feeling sick and full of dread.

Will I make it to my house?
I'm just glad I'm not a mouse!

Ann Polkins

NOTHING LEFT TO SAY

Exchanging comments about the weather
Left me wondering how we had ever
Found enough in common
To have ever fallen in love.
And trying as hard as you might
You could not stop the conversation
From getting too polite,
Superficial, meaningless and mundane.
We parted with an affectionless embrace,
You trying to hide from your face
The relief you felt.
(That we were unlikely to ever meet again)
And as we parted I wondered this -
Were we ever more than intimate strangers
Even when we kissed,
And was your love making
A mere masquerade?
Is this, I wonder, how it always ends,
Sometime lovers becoming shallow friends ...
With nothing left to say?

Paul Farmer

WE ARE ONE

Towering, crashing, cold blue seas,
Freezing ice, floating,
Melting into warm, sunlit waters
Castaway on deserted shores,
Our thoughts washed away with the tide,
Our bodies warmed by the sun.
We are one.

Carol Ivens

DON'T DESPAIR

Behind the clouds
The sun still shines
Although it's out of view
And when the clouds begin to move
The sun comes shining through

So don't despair
Or have a care
When you can't see your way
Just look up and you will see
The clouds have gone away

Sometimes our thoughts
Are like the clouds
They do get in the way
And then we worry needlessly
And that can spoil our day

Louis Robert Early

DESTINATION HEAVEN

A dream slips in beside me,
Before I realise,
Destination heaven,
First stop, paradise.

No eyes ever looked so deep before,
Awakening feelings, wanting more,
Lips seducing, stealing my heart,
If I wake up now I'll fall apart,
So I let my sleepy eyes dream on,
Before my mind sees that you've gone.

As your skin touches mine,
And our bodies entwine,
I hear those violins
And angels on guitars,
You gave me a dream to dream,
The sun, the moon and the stars.

A dream slips in beside me,
Every time I close my eyes,
Destination heaven,
First stop, paradise.

Jacqueline C Rolfe

THE ROSE

For sheer beauty, I don't suppose,
There isn't any flower as beautiful as a rose.
Each petal beautifully moulded,
From leaf to stem, exquisitely folded,
Alas of course, there is a thorn,
On many a finger it has been torn,
Perhaps there is a moral to tell,
A flower so delicate, can be sharp as well.

Gladys Gale

Gladys Gale said: "I am a senior citizen and I have made writing poems a hobby since being widowed 19 years ago. Since then, I have written my memoirs and my wartime experiences in the WAAF. I am blessed with three sons, six grandsons, four granddaughters, four great-grandsons and a great-granddaughter who I see regularly. They bring happiness into my life."

RINGS

Rings rings and other things,
The telephone rings,
A smile it brings,
Is it for me?
Is it for me?
No,
It's for my family,
Rings, rings.

Tony O'Brien

FOOTPRINTS

In the middle of my kitchen floor
There's a bag of opened flour,
White footprints through my house
That I will have to follow,
Handprints on the table,
And the kitchen door,
Along the hallway,
Up the stairs,
Into a little person's room.
Under the bed there are giggles,
So I take a look and smile,
Innocent eyes stare back at me,
So I stop and talk a while.
At last I move,
A small hand in mine,
To follow the footprints
Back to the kitchen,
To where it all began.

Jeanette Homewood

WASHING DAY

Monday is washing day
Soak the clothes in the tub
With bare hands rub and scrub
Sunlight soap and lots of suds
Is this enough to remove the mud
All the whites in the copper
Boiling now good and proper
Time to rinse in the sink
Washing day, it just stinks
To squeeze the water out the clothes
In the mangle they must go
In one end and out the other
Flat as a pancake, said my mother
Peg them on the washing line
A day's work done just in time
Times have changed, it's now washing automatic
Thank goodness for that, I'm just ecstatic

Patricia Blackett

NATURE'S BEAUTY QUEEN

The sunset was low,
As was my mood,
Until I saw God's beautiful scene,
The opulent colours made me feel so serene,
I gave thanks to God,
And Mother Nature too,
For making the sunset their beauty queen.

Elaine McSporran

VIETNAM '98

This is something I learned in 'Nam,
back in '98.
How to smoke through a rifle barrel
and put it down butt first,
So you don't ruin the end sight.
And how to survive
The sniper in the window
(either charge or go through smoke.)
How to pick my spot on the last chopper out
And how,
Though I walk through the valley of death
I will trust the whistling Jekyll rather than
Backup needed on the f****ing double.
How to spot where I shouldn't have been
When to cut the losses
When to hit the surf.

Vietnam '98.
Me love you long time.

Joshua Piercey

Dedicated to Alex Garland for pointing out the glamour.

SOCIAL SERVICES

You said we'd been treated badly,
An apology we were due,
But that was over two months ago,
And we've still heard nothing from you.

You promised a new core assessment,
To replace the one that was fudged,
But we waited six weeks for a visit ,
Did that leave enough time to be judged?

You appointed a social worker
Who was booked for medical leave,
If the case against us had been valid,
You'd have left a child to grieve.

You said we'd have all the papers,
Four days to read them, we'd get,
But it's only three days to the meeting,
And we haven't heard anything yet.

We are the people who pay you,
You're supposed to work with us,
If you'd received such bad service,
Wouldn't you make a fuss?

Christabel Rosina Hedges

A LIGHT THOUGHT

Insistent fluorescent will tire the mind,
Constant candescent can render one blind.
But solescent when present I think you will find.
The prognosis is doses,
Through shades of roses,
Tints of ochre,
Hues of mocha.
And graphite suffices the jocular ocular,
Safe in the shadow behind.

Philip Sanderson

THE SHEARERS

Looking down I cannot see my feet
The hair on my chest has grown
So long and bulky this winter
I'm sure it's due to global warming.
How much longer do we have to wait
For the shearers to arrive?
Nice chaps, they come from Australia
Wherever that may be.
The sun is beating down making me hot,
I cannot wait to feel a cool breeze
Blowing down my back to make me
Want to jump and skip.
When we are taken into the shed
We're a little nervous, but the shearers'
Skilled hands have us in position - then
In a few minutes the old coat is off,
Rolled up and pushed to one side.
Then we are free of all that wool
It feels so good we want the world to know
Look I can see my feet again.

Gillian Whittome

GOODNIGHT BOXES

Today
I made
a box inside my head
and named it *yours* in red
I filled it up with you
and moody saxophone blues,
I adorned my box in ribbons
made from the kisses you'd given
to me
one anniversary.
I carved it from a lime tree
and darling-do-you-love-me's.
I stuffed it full of your caress
and a sneeze that you had once blessed.
I sprinkled on some powdered forever
and signed it us together.
I locked it shut with a late night prayer
and asked the Lord that you'd be there
When I awake
tomorrow.

Daniella Maison

Born in Buckinghamshire, **Daniella Maison** describes her style as reflective, soulful, nostalgic and moody. "I came to be a writer the moment I used creativity to put a spin on the world around me. This produced my first poem when I was six years-old," she remarked. "I would like to be remembered for making a positive difference in the world and I am currently in the final stages of completing master of arts degree in medieval literature. After this I hope to be a full-time writer." Aged 25, Daniella has written a short story and many poems.

LADYBIRD

In your polkadot dress so red,
You look very smart it must be said.
Pretty little bug, small and sweet,
Looking good from your head to your feet.
Folks say to you a little rhyme,
That's been around for a very long time.
Ladybird, ladybird fly away,
Your house is on fire, that's what they say
So as quickly off you fly,
I wave to you a fond goodbye.

June Lilian Downey

POWER IN THE INK

There is power in the pen
Dip in ink and then
Write a line or ten
There is power in the pen.

There is power in the arm
To fight or to disarm
To support or shield from harm
There is power in the arm.

There is power in the think
To win and not kick up a stink
To sway or move from brink
To find Mensa's missing link.

To influence, to have your say
To claim your rights, to seize the day
If not with fist, with pen you may
There is power in the ink, today.

Charlotte Harris

COUNTRYSIDE GIRL

I'd wander my own path,
I'd walk country stiles.
Thinking my way,
I'd be carried for miles.
Barefoot through the fields,
I didn't have a care.
Bluebells and buttercups,
With clouds in the air.

Well that's all changed
Now that I see
My entire world
Completely differently.
I've had to grow up,
It's expected of me,
But my new world,
It's just not me.

I now only visit
My fields in my dreams,
Where I used to wander
Through forests and streams.
I wish I could go back
To the great outside,
Because I'll always be
A girl of the countryside.

Louise Elliott

TEARS

If only tears could quell the pain,
That heartbreak brings, alas in vain,
The tears still fall though years have gone,
Hurt, sadness, and grief felt still goes on,
Time heals all, or so they say,
No, nothing takes all pain away,
So as we stand, with heads held high,
And say once more a fond goodbye,
Outside we show our love and pride,
Within we hide a heart that's died.

Sylvia M Blackwell

MY 2CV

Little Citroen, funny car
How I wonder what you are
Not a *Roller* out of reach
Not a *Buggy* for the beach
Not a Porsche or Beetle Bug
More an upright kind of slug.
A little facelift, nip and tuck
At your best you're just a duck
No great beauty have we here
A little bit quirky and a wee bit queer.
Though not a pretty sight to see
You are always tops with me
You raise a smile along the road
Putting paid to Highway Code
One day when I'm rich not poor
I'll turn you into a four by four.

Sheila Webb

MAYTIME

If you had to pay
Everyday
Throughout May
For the white lace heads
That line the kerb
Together with grass and herb,
And thick white blossom
To drape the hedge
With such density on
Hawthorn's tree,
Just be thankful,
Look and see,
It's worth a fortune
And we get it for free.

Dorinda Smith

TIMMY'S LAST FAREWELL

A darling little kitten, not much bigger than his head,
who used to love fish and chicken, when he was being fed.
In spring, summer and autumn, there would be Timmy,
in between the flowers, rolled up and fast asleep.
His favourite spot would be near the old pear tree.
Whenever he was poorly we would take him to the vet,
he gave us love and lots of joy, our darling tabby boy.
When years passed by and Timmy grew old,
and that spring day, when we were told,
the time had come to bid Timmy farewell,
it broke our hearts and we cried.
We loved and missed him so, more than words could say.
On that fateful spring day, we put flowers on the grave,
where our Timmy lay,
near by, his favourite spot.

Mary Flower

TOO BANAL?

Snatching a falling leaf
He felt a splinter of memory
In his frozen hand
A chapter of a story too banal
Yet impossible to comprehend

Radek Glabazna

WHEN I PASS

Cry at my graveside then wipe them away
because when you leave it's party time OK.
I may have gone but you're still around
so I don't want to hear that weeping sound.
Remember the good times and none of the bad
then this way you'll never be sad.
Many years you've had with me
now up above is where I must be.
When on earth I forever vowed
to try and make my loved ones proud.
Although I've done wrong I hope I've done right
and left you all with a little light.
I only wish I could give you a sign
but I promise I'll look in from time to time.
I hope I'm looking down and not looking up
because constant neck cramp would really suck.
So to all my loved ones this is farewell
I'll be at the gates when you ring the bell.

Sadie Jerrim

EARLY MORNING ENCOUNTER

Dawn misty and dull across the wide field
is pierced by sudden light. I see now
what was before invisible: a deer
delicately stepping from left to right.
Its fine head turns to look at me; breathing
quietly it moves again, then gathers
pace, and bounds beyond my sight.

Juliet Close

MEMORIES OF A LEFTY

I've been left handed all my life, sometimes it's been a
curse, and when I used my right hand it just made matters
worse.
I wasn't allowed a biro back when I was at school
I had to use a fountain pen, that was the golden rule.
But writing with a fountain pen was somewhat of a drudge
Because anything I'd written immediately got smudged.

School dinners though were something else they tried to
make me change,
Put your spoon into your *write* hand boy, no wonder I'm
deranged.
I'd grit my teeth and glare at them, obscenities I'd mutter,
Treating children like they did could leave them with a
stutter.
Ask anyone that stammers in this green and pleasant land
And if they're being truthful they'd say blame my left hand.

Gerald Harrold

VIEWPOINT

As I turn the corner from Crookhorn Lane,
I'm overwhelmed by the beauty once again,
From my vantage point I see the city unfold,
A panoramic view, a pleasure to behold.

The changing weather brings contrasting light,
And each day brings a different sight,
Threatening clouds scudding through the sky,
Create a dramatic scene as I pass by.

When the sun shines on a glistening sea,
A truly magnificent scene I see.
And as darkness descends on a winter's night,
The city is ablaze with flickering light.

Far in the distance I can see the docks,
There are church spires, houses and tower blocks.
Against the backdrop of a cloudless sky,
In the gentle breeze white sails glide by.

Now the resplendent Spinnaker Tower
Signals Portsmouth's mighty naval power,
And by boldly reaching high up above,
Adds a landmark to the view I love.

Doreen Bowers

Born in East London, **Doreen Bowers** has interests including reading, crosswords, poetry and writing. "I started writing poetry in 1942 and my work is influenced by my late father who enjoyed quoting poetry," she remarked. "I would describe my style as easy reading and I would like to be remembered as an author and poet" Aged 76, Doreen is retired and has an ambition to finish and publish her own novel. She is a widow with a daughter and two grandchildren."

THE SOMERSET YEOMAN

At the age of twenty-three he left
The animals, dirt and fields
To become a soldier.
Dressed in a uniform to be proud of
A gun by his side
Sent to France to be killed in an orchard
Shot by a farmer in uniform.

Debra Wood

NEW LIFE

On a bright cloudless day
Along the winding lane, we wended our way
In the distance a loud moo-ing we heard.
We held our breath, for over the hedge
A large, black, shiny cow had given birth
To a fresh, new, brown and white precious bundle.
As it opened its eyes and took its first breath,
The trees waved a welcome
The bright sun smiled down.
Proud mother cow gently licked, prodded and pushed
Until...
Teetering and wobbling the calf stood,
Walked on spindly legs,
Took milk from her teats.
How privileged we felt to witness such joy.
Everyday now, at that spot we stare in awe
Thank you God for your wonderful world.

Gillian Hitchens

MY GARDEN

I work hard in my garden
It gives me backache, and a glow
To see the things I've planted, flourish and to grow
No matter how I try, I just cannot find the time
To weed, water, feed and hoe round every plant of mine.
My flowers are quite colourful, beautiful, although
Not quite up to standard for the Chelsea Flower Show
The flowers shown at Chelsea really are sublime
But I bet there's not a thistle there quite as good as mine.

Margaret Murray

THE CUCKOO

Where is that elusive harbinger
Who heralded once our summer days
In May or June from Pelham Woods
Beyond the fragile bluebell haze?
Now only the pigeons emulate his call
Deceptive imitators, all.

Now felled the ash and sycamore
Potatoes planted where the shy bird sang
While coal black crows patrol the track
Where his dual note often rang
Still the bridal may stars the sky
But we listen in vain for his yearly cry.

No foster nests are needed now
For no cuckoo haunts the hidden bough.

Paula Stewart

PURRFECT MOMENTS

Something fishy, cod or plaice
Canned or packeted, you choose boys.
Shrimp or sardine, tuna, dace
We're hunting for your choice.

By the cat food shelves we pause
Whilst at home they stretch their claws.
Beside warm radiators rest
Confident we'll buy the best.

When we bought canned, they changed their tastes
Two turned up their purrfect noses,
What they don't like goes to waste
We'll cook some wet fish, one supposes.

Cats are loving, cats are fickle
Turn upside down, ask for a tickle.
But if the newspapers we read
They walk across, demand a feed.

Patricia Ross

Born in Hull, **Patricia Ross** has interests including caravanning, gardening, caring for cats and painting. "At the age of 15 I was a freelance correspondent for the local newspaper which started my writing career," she explained. "I would like to be remembered as a local historian, a helpful tutor of dyslexic students and a loyal member of Chichester folk song club," she explained. "I am a 77 year-old author and teacher and the person I would most like to meet is the Queen as I admire her energy and enthusiasm." Patricia is married to John and together they have six children and nine grandchildren.

FOREST

The mouths of birds and bees
Have words that float amongst the trees,
The gifted mind can reach
To find them 'midst the canopies.

A beautiful but lonely song
Lays bare the inner soul
of all who hear, and see how dear
The forest mankind stole.

Dan Bierton

INFERNAL

A new energy
So powerful, that I have no control.
A burning sensation; that turned my heart charcoal black
And a sight, of which only sees demons
And humans doing evil sinnings, that I;
In all damnation I corrupt, with poisonous words
And misleading thoughts.
Just watching the world fall in disbelief.

No one knows, because I disappear in the mist of night,
For the evidence left; the symbolic sign,
Number 666, for I am the leading ark Angel of Lucifer; my
lord
And my destiny, my mission, my life is for hell to be
unleashed and watch God worshippers bow to my master.
Lucifer!

David A M Shergold

KYMBA

I feel your spirit on the breeze
It moves me
The wind that gently stirs the trees
Soothes me
I long to hold you, but your form eludes me
Memory cannot replace that, which death took from me

The waves that lap the sun warmed shore
Whisper your name
Then return, gone forever more
Drifting on the timeless tides
Restless spirit, peaceful rides

You loved to play
You gave it all
And then you left us
Lost, adrift, alone
Enriched by every precious, cherished moment
But how can we go on?
Strong and brave, valiant and true
The same as our example, set by you.

Carole Jones

THE NUDIST

Here I sit, pink and bare,
For I have no clothes to wear.
I do not wear slacks, nor blouses or shirts,
Dungarees, dresses or even skirts.
I don't agree with clothing as it covers my fine self
And all of the fresh air is good for my health.
Yes, people do stop and stare
When they see my pubic hair.
But I just grin and give them a wave,
And introduce myself, *Hi, I'm Dave.*

Jessica Burton

DARK STAR

Hold my hand up to the light,
Knowing soon the sun will find the night.
As sure as Mrs Moon ne'er sees the day,
I still can't seem to find my way.
Through bracken and briar,
My soul flies higher,
'Till it rests upon stars and sun,
Then back down here I quickly run.
Laughter, love, friends and light,
Still I rejoice in the passionate night.
My knight in shining armour will save the day,
Though many dragons he has to slay.
And through the wintering, wildish dream
I will run on and down to the stream.
As many times as I've seen Mars,
I'll always remember your dark stars.

Sahna Jubb

THINKING OF JACQUELINE

Always thinking of Jacqueline in Heaven above
We send to our daughter an abundance of love
The big C has taken our Jacqueline from us
But she was so brave and left without fuss.
She fought for her life and never gave in
Her character shone from without and within.

We look to the night sky, stars twinkle and shine
We know she's so happy and everything's fine.

Jacqueline loved to have fun, to party and dance
She also was caring and left nothing to chance
She had a spring in her step and a gleam in her eye
One thing's for certain, she never was shy.

Sometimes when we think of what might have been
The tears tumble down but they are not seen
So we look on the bright side and forget when we cried
And think of our Jacqueline who filled us with pride.

Colin Plumley

OLD WINCHESTER HILL

Bees buzzing,
Birds singing,
Butterflies dancing,
Gorse blooming.
Sun shining,
Grass growing,
Sheep grazing,
Dad snoozing,
Me reading,
Nothing doing,
Yet everything living
On old Winchester hill.

Dorothy Jeram

GOD

That being which so mystically serene
Everywhere is God on all life's scenes
Comprehend can we not fully
Although perhaps we can't prove it scientifically
Yet God is mystically serene.

God is in the tree, flower, animal, sea, mountain, sand,
Understanding life's strife, and the music of the band
Yes, he's in all that wonderful world of human nature too
Guiding people what they can or cannot do.

God is in every bird flying in the sky
In a child's play and a baby's cry
In love we see him best of all
If it's God we love, life's a sure treasure
To one and all.

Elizabeth A Sander

MOONLIT ANDOVER

The skies over my town are filled with joy tonight, and every night.
As the sun sets over Andover, the stars are coming out, and the moon is shining.
I tread these streets that I have walked a thousand times before.
I feel hope and warmth, community.
And a vision of a better life rises into the dark.

Amy Townsend

Born in Winchester **Amy Townsend** has interests including reading, writing, playing the guitar and horse riding. "When I was about seven I wrote my first story to impress my friends. I loved it and I have been writing ever since," she remarked. "My work is influenced by the poet Julia Rhiain Phillips and I would describe my style as gentle though occasionally dark and twisted. I would like to be remembered as someone's favourite author." Aged 15, Amy is a student with an ambition to become a bestselling author. The person she would most like to meet is the author Chris Woodings.

KISSING

I love the way you kiss me,
And run your fingers through my hair.
Kissing is so wonderful, and
Something you can share.

Your lips are smooth and silky,
And taste so very sweet.
I know when they are pouted
I'm in for such a treat.

I'd like to thank the person,
For whoever invented kissing.
If they haven't tried it,
They don't know what they're missing.

Sarah Grant

CHANDLER'S FORD

Chandler's Ford, a suburban sprawl
Spreading and sprawling where green fields once bloomed.
Community split, divided, commuted
Rich from both parents working.
What can one say about Chandler's Ford?
Our train station is walkable, a link with the world.
Our schools are to envy, choices for all
From infant to adult, nurtured and cared.
We boast parks and oak trees,
Here from Chandler's Ford's past,
Shops for the best and churches for all.
The weather is clement
All year round.
Chandler's Ford is
A gem to be found.

Tessa Askew

DO NOT DISTURB

I cannot take your call right now,
So please put down your phone,
You can find me in a certain place,
But you'll find me all alone.

It's cold and dark and miserable,
With no friends to see,
This place is a place for reflection,
This place is a place for me.

It's not a room, or a street or a corner,
I am in no place that is real,
I am lonely, not independent,
I am too numb to feel.

I do not deserve an escape route,
No ropes, no ladders, no friends.
Because the longer I stay in this place,
The sooner my journey ends.

Claire Wakefield

THE COMMUTER

Standing on a train,
Crammed against the doors,
Looking out the windows,
Is this what life is for?

The cemetery passes by,
Ablaze with grass and flowers,
People lying down forever,
Eternity on the hour.

One day in the future,
I won't need the fare,
I'll just watch the trains go by,
While I'm a-lying there.

Peter Dickerson

FIRST SNOW

The finger of heaven drops
Frost below on sleeping earth
So we awake to a white world
So still and quiet as snow falls
Gently, like swans' feathers
I wish the world would be
Bathed in peace, as this
Illusionary glimpse of calm;
Before man's bustle
Leaves its mark of discord
In war, in rage, in noise
Let's have laughter and love
On earth, from a heavenly dove
Spreading its white wings
Over a sleeping world

Betty Shipway

BRENDA

Brenda is her name,
With her I play a little game,
With her I will flirt,
As she's ironing my shirt.

As she makes my bed,
I get ideas in my head,
I will help her make my bed,
But I make a cup of tea instead.

Ireland has forty shades of green,
Most of which I have seen,
Brenda too has eyes of green,
Most beautiful eyes I have seen.

But in spite of all my schemes,
And of all my daydreams,
Alas, alas, it now seems,
I can only love her in my dreams.

Philip Reynolds

MY DAD

I want my dad
Like I once had
To have and to hold
Until I get old.

I need to see him and hear him I wish
But my dad just went with a sudden swish
I wish he was here for me to see
So then with him I could be.

When bad things happen I always cry
But when he went I really thought I would die
We are separated in reality
But in my heart we will never be.

Nicky Jones

RETROSPECTION

On my own, just standing here,
I feel her close, another near,
Then turning round, I see myself
But I'm not me, I'm someone else.

Viewing all the secrets I have left behind,
Imaginative wanderings of a child's happy mind.

Reflections of a chapter gone.
Visions of all that I've done,
Travels in a time device
Memories of a younger life.

Private thoughts alone, that none can understand,
Fascinating walks into another's fairy land.

Charlie Annalls

UN-CHRISTIAN

This boy walks on, ignoring the jokes
from those beasts with hearts of cold,
burning him by mouth with bursts of frozen flame
and he walks on, ignoring.
Day by day, this boy endures
the unkind, un-Christian works of poison-dipped tongues.
He cannot choke their fire
or choke his own,
he must walk on, ignoring
though it's obvious to me
he's crying inside.
And I leave well alone. A fool.
Then, at last, I choose to comfort him,
abandon the cold, embrace the warm,
and leave behind the Satan's ones
where, once, I did fit in.
The air is damp as I reach for him,
a cold, crisp wind blows as I reach to dry his tears
and touch the frozen image in the mirror.

Christopher Berry

MY SPECIAL PLACE

I have a special place I sometimes go,
It's only mine, a place no others know.

It's my secret beach in a far-off land,
Where I sit on the warm, golden sand.

With bright blue seas and always sunny days,
It's such a beautiful place in so many ways.

I sit with the sand between my toes
As I watch the breaking waves go to and fro.

It's so peaceful and quiet with no sound but the waves,
It's such a dreamy place, it's like a daze.

I go there to relax and rest my mind,
In my special place all is always fine.

But back to reality I always have to go,
But I know I can return when the stress starts to show.

Emma Gray

LOST FOR WORDS

Lost for words inner thoughts as a child I did grow
of those that once filled me with grief and sorrow.
I found that I felt different from others around me
what was wrong with me but what was right to me
at an age of inexperience could not understand
why not? Not everything was so grand
yes lost for words fear from others not understanding.

But now of an age I am to see the rights and wrongs cast
of others that feared me and my mother, father since
passed
all peaceful and calm as I hand-signed for the last time
over my parents graves for they were always lost for words
they were deaf you see as I wept in that time
peace and tranquil of the graveyard I'm not lost for words
but to hold my life so dear now experienced understanding.

Charles Adams

Dedicated to my mother, father and nan, the world that they lived, different from others, I'm not Lost For Words.

COCKY LITTLE MATE

Every single morning,
She comes to the kitchen door,
I throw her out a custard cream
And then she wants some more.
Until I throw her out a biscuit
She'll just stand and wait,
My little robin red-breast
My cocky little mate.

Harold Plecker

GETTING FIT

Is it too late to join a gym
And get myself healthy and fit?
Will all the others be gorgeous and slim
While I stand there and feel like a twit?
Will my old body stand up to the strain?
Will my back and my thighs give me gip?
Or will I adapt and become agile and lithe,
With a tum that's had a tuck and a nip?
The thought of the treadmill just makes me squirm,
And I dream about weights in the night.
Will my arms lose the flab
And my skin look less drab?
When I'm tightened and toned and don't hurt.
Will my boobs get a lift?
And my body weight shift?
Will my bum become firmed-up and pert?
But at sixty nine, I think I'm just fine,
Over the hill maybe, but alright.

Maureen Sibley

REFLECTIONS

I'm looking out the window,
What do I see?
I see a reflection,
A reflection of me.
I'm looking out the window,
There's nobody about.
I get so very lonely,
I feel I could shout.
I'm looking out the window,
At least I'm not alone.
There's always that reflection,
So I'm never on my own.
I'm looking out the window,
It's very late you know.
I think it must be bedtime,
So it's time for us to go.
When I wake tomorrow,
I wonder what I'll see.
Will my reflection still
Be looking back at me?

Lilian Buckland

THE SMOTHERING TIDE

As the sun dips out of sight,
Drive your car to the beach tonight.
As the sun dips out of sight,
Take a walk to the beach tonight.

Lights sparkle on the waves that roar,
From ships headed for a different shore.
The sea, and the smothering tide,
Let it take us where we can hide.

Pictured by a palm tree in the sand,
As we get stoned and crack a can.
Stop and find a pretty shell for her,
You know she's in love with you, man.

It's wonderful to be alone,
Stars sparkle in the sky at night.
Oh, just stay there on your own,
Because I'll think of you tonight.

Aaron Richards

SOLD OUT

A time for selling,
Of goods so cheap,
Of ideals and passions
Laid at my dad's feet.

I've sold the lot, he said,
As I watched him there,
With bright new shoes
And vacant stare.

It's best all gone,
He replied once more,
I turned and gently
Closed the door.

Nothing could wake him,
From that dreadful sleep.
He'd left and gone,
Sold out so cheap.

I sighed, and turned to watch the sky,
In deepest tranquil blue sublime.
How dare the sun decide to shine
And mock this fatal, fragile, mind.

Henry Small

OUR CHILDREN

God gives us children
With His love
To treat them with love and care,

And if it's abuse to a child
You're thinking of doing
Don't you dare.

Better you go your own way
And leave the children to live
To see another day.

Margaret Alexander

MR AVERAGE

I think of myself as an average man;
no thrills, no spills.
I have no special talents, though I do
join in on occasional karaoke with a pint
in the local pub,
Go home to where my wife cooks my grub.
I have just three children, two sons and a daughter.
My daughter doesn't drink tea or coffee,
she'd rather just drink water.
Just love to go to church with my kids and wife,
And I just love the quiet life.
On occasional parties I might just want to go,
Build a snowman with my daughter and with some snow.
Christmas is just so special to me, with everything which
just goes with it around our tree.
I'm not a rich man but it doesn't just interest me.
I'm just this man, Mr Average, pleased to be just me.

Cliff Howe

BROTHER

As I remember our time together,
I do not feel so sad,
You have always been there for me,
Even when times were bad.

You gave me a shoulder to cry on,
And the strength to see me through,
For all your generosity,
I want to say, thank you.

Thank you for being my brother,
A kind and loving man,
All the times they said I couldn't
You always said *you can.*

Your belief in me was tremendous,
It made me feel so strong,
And with you there to guide me,
I felt I could do no wrong.

The love I have is endless,
For you, my brother dear,
Even when my time has come,
I will always feel you near.

Vicki Lewis

WHO APES WHO?

How dare they say we are distant kin,
When all they do is war and sin.
We don't behave like men,
That horrible race of Homosapien.

When have you ever seen us steal?
Okay, just a piece of banana peel.
Do we battle over what we see?
Sure, but only if it's our territory.

Do we pollute our sacred land?
We chew the leaves and dig the sand.
And do we have sex when incomplete?
Well only when our mate's not on heat.

So if you think only the fittest survive,
How come we are still alive?
For if we were not up to scratch,
Then why weren't we soon dispatched?

If humans think they are the best
And we only grunt and beat our chest,
Just think who is to blame,
Aren't we all just the same?

Mankind ... The pinnacle of evolution?
Mr Darwin ... What a crazy solution!

Linda Fellows

Linda Fellows said: "I have only recently started to write poetry. I am also an artist who specialises in pyrography. I usually write about what moves me, to personal emotion and sometimes topical issues like the above poem. I'm unusual in my belief that evolution is false, and although written in a humorous way, I do believe what I have stated in my poem! I also create Sapphic poems and artwork."

SEASONS

If I could choose a season,
It would not be an easy thing.
They all have their blessings,
With the colours that they bring.
The summer roses, the heavenly perfume,
The hazy nights, the stars, the moon.
The winter sparkle, the dazzle of snow,
The clean, bright mornings, the fires that glow.
Then autumn with the leaves that fall,
The reds, the golds, I love them all.
But then the buds, the birds that sing,
And best of all, another spring.

Tricia Howard

GLOBAL WARMING

Is global warming down to us
Why do we make such a fuss
In our cars and on the bus
Aeroplanes flying over us

Has this happened all before
Should we believe it anymore
In my opinion excuse the pun
The culprit could be the sun

So it would be nice if all the glaciers stay frozen ice
And the mighty current of the Gulf stream
Doesn't evaporate into steam

I agree we should not relax or we may pay a heavier tax
So from today let's hope and pray
Global warming's not here to stay

Alan Smith

JUST ONE OF MY LITTLE SPELLS, DEAR

The tired lady of the house slumped down
I'm weary wearing this housekeeping crown
Maybe a good fairy will wave her wand, she sighed
Eyes drooping in half sleep she fantasised

Bewitched casting spells as her nose twitched
Housework by one was done, clothes stitched
Beds made, cupboards sorted, washing on the line
What else shall I do with my time?

With a nose twitch the garden was neat
Next stop the shops, not on her feet
A magical sneeze bore her there on a breeze
Inviting friends back home for cream teas

Her guests so quiet, no one was at ease
So spick and span, atmosphere to freeze
How come our friend is suddenly Mrs Perfect
Startled, the hostess awoke, deciding to twitch wasn't
worth it

Real friends are forever she thought
Work is character building, life's battles to be fought
That's not to say the itch to twitch will go away
She would dream about it another day

Wendy Greenhill

NEAR WHERE I LIVE

Near where I live is Cole Green way
It is the place where people love to walk and play.
It used to be an old railway line
Now they've taken the tracks up, so that is fine.

Down the road there is a wood
Full of animals and trees, and that is good.
Down the hill there is Letty Green
Where nice houses have got to be seen.

With fields and farmland all around
You can see and hear wildlife, if you are outward bound.
It is good to live in a rural location
But it is a shame that we no longer have a station.

Peter Stannard

WESLEY AND HIS COLD

My name is Wesley and I've got a cold
My skin is all wrinkly, and I look so old
There's no one to love me or give me a cuddle
My nose is all blocked and my head's in a fuddle

Nobody loves me because I've got a germ
Nobody loves me anyway because I'm a worm
A worm with a germ is strictly taboo
I bet you're glad you're not me, aren't you?

I'm here in my worm hole and I'm freezing
Sniffling and snuffling, snitching and sneezing
Here in my worm hole, all on my own
I'm a worm with a germ and I'm all alone

Ann Rogers

SUMMER IN BAYSWATER

7:00pm.
Lots of people.
Some look like they've just left work,
others all dressed up for a night out.

A woman walks past me in a sequinned top;
a multicolored butterfly spread across her chest.

I look up to the first floor of a white painted house,
to see two men and a woman on the balcony.
One man casually sits astride the balustrade drinking beer.
I hear their laughter.

I walk on and pass a group of men in their twenties,
Standing on the pavement just talking.
Seemingly pleased to be anywhere,
provided they're in each other's company.

A hot evening to end a hot day.
Everyone seems happier now that it's summer again.
Each man a friend of all others.
This is how it should be always.
No more wars, no more hatred.
Just endless, beautiful, summer evenings in Bayswater.

Paula Harvey

Dedicated to my father, Les Facey.

RUSH

Are we nearly there, Mum,
are we nearly there?

Children's voices whine.
Tense hands grip steering wheel
as distracted mother attempts
to negotiate rush-hour traffic.

Soon, her short answer
bites. She flicks her hair,
glances at her reflection,
doesn't see the lorry turn.

Freeze-framed silence numbs,
before brakes screech,
metals grind. Over the cacophony
a ghostly echo reverberates.

Are we nearly there, Mum,
are we nearly there?

Penny Smith

NOT FOR ME

Not for me that perfect garden of today,
Gravel, wood chips and slabs paving the way.
The patio and the barbecue that are a must,
And a water feature too, I trust.
But a country garden filled with haphazard colours and scents,
From spade work hours to give pleasure well meant.

No neat rows of plants, just a rambling way,
Through sweet-peas, honeysuckle and roses in abandoned array.
No special features cast in cement or brick,
But a sea of wafting silky poppies to do the trick
Of drawing in the breath and catching the eye,
Like an artist's palate beneath a blue sky.

A wooden bench beneath a tree,
Sunlight glinting through leaves that dapple me.
A place to think, to dream, or hide away,
And just enjoy a summer's day.

Freda Rudman

IN TRANSITION

Speak to me
of things inspiring
lift my soul
for all to see
let my heart
sing out rejoicing
of the love
you have for me

Bide my time
whilst understanding
washes, soothes
my broken heart
pray forgive those
not so kindly
memories hope
soon to depart

Heal me Father
hear me crying
new life bring me
old one dying

Brenda Evans

SHORT STORY FOR LANGUAGE STUDENTS

Going out
going steady
going together
he's going
what's going on now?
An ongoing story

Felicity Jenkins

IF I WASN'T ME THEN WHO WOULD I BE?

A sexy dancer in a far away Kasbah,
A spinsterish lady entertaining ma and pa,
A blue stocking knee deep in complicated books,
A model relying simply on good looks,
A fiery flamenco dancer whose soul is pure fire,
A lady of the night sophisticated and purely for hire,
An artist finding new things to inspire,
A nun singing praises to God in high,
Or a day dreaming dolly watching the world pass by,
Armchair explorer and traveller too,
So many things to see and do.

Sandra Wilkes

EVERYTHING

A thousand words are not enough to say how much you mean to me,
But one is *everything*.
It's you who makes me sing,
I'm free as a bird on the wing.

No one can hear the sounds,
But deep inside, my heart pounds.
I know that I am yours, and you'll be mine,
Until the very end of time.

With you I will always walk,
I know you listen when I talk.
When I don't know what to do,
I know I can always turn to you.

You accept me, happy or sad,
You understand when things make me mad.
You cover me with love,
I'm the hand and you're the glove.

I can't wait to see your face,
So, for now, I'll live in your grace.

Stephanie Wilson

UNFOLDS HER AS A FLOWER

As simple as a breath he unfolds her as a flower
Then sweeps her in his arms
He dies for just one hour

Journeys through her heart to walk the fields of fire
Determined to be strong upon the beast of sorrow

He's found her in the garden by the beaten wood
As gentle as a flower he lifts her in his hold

Her every limb is soft, lying in his power
And to the lake he goes to drench her in this hour

He lays her by the rocks and watches in his sorrow
To play the harp of love and kiss her by the hour

His time has returned so now he must flower
And through the lake he glides and holds her with his power

And as she awakes his eyes begin to flower

Into her heart he breaks
And dies within in his sorrow

Sandra Whelan

NO GOODBYES

For us, my dear friend,
The time is now here.
For us to split paths,
And hold back our fear.

We will see each other
Again, this is true.
And one thing's for certain,
I won't forget you.

We both laughed so hard,
That tears filled our eyes.
The tears of a friendship
That has no goodbyes.

The friendship we have
Has always been strong.
I know this because
We've lasted so long.

To you, this may feel
Like one long goodbye.
But we'll last forever
As friends, you and I.

Elaina Swiffen

HELDER (HELDAIR)

What, I hear you ask, can be the reason for this rhyme?
It really is quite simple, so if you have the time,
I'll tell you about the story of this chap here, full of flair,
To put it in a nutshell, he's *a waiter extraordinaire*

He runs this place unaided, and when he gets quite busy,
He never flaps or gets uptight, he's never in a tizzy,
When he takes your order, he'll smile and say *amigos,*
He doesn't seem to have a care, but if he does, it never
shows.

You'll find it such a pleasure to see his happy face,
Smiling eyes that welcome you, and character full of grace,
This guy is really something else, for him I'm full of praise,
He's made me feel so welcome here for many, many days.

If you're staying in Tavira, and want food prepared with
care,
Come eat here at *The Bica* and meet our friend Helder.

Sally-Ann Deakin

DARTMOUTH REGATTA

Dartmouth regatta is over
The last of the fireworks has died,
The arrows have roared back over the hill.
And the frigates gone out on the tide.
The fair with its music a-booming,
Has packed up and gone on its way.
The rowers and racers and rafters,
Have all had to call it a day.
Dartmouth regatta is over.
The last of the fireworks has died,
The arrows have roared back over the hill
And the frigates gone out on the tide.

Barbara Featherstone

THE MAC AND I (BY ROYAL APPOINTMENT)

The Queen we met on our special day,
But not a hand on *the mac* did lay.
It was a little chat and a wonderful smile,
Did it really happen that she stopped a while?

In coat and hat of royal blue,
Us in Sunday best, as good as new.
Hats and all, what a sight we made,
'Twill be the talk of our decade.

Despite the rain, and umbrellas at the ready,
The *mac* and I stood firm and steady.
So back to the coaches went one and all,
Where the poor old *mac* was rolled up small.

Jean Gillmore

DIED TODAY

Died today, he died today,
My friend, who would always say,
Don't give up, there's always hope,
Even on this boggy slope.

Died today, he died today,
Another brave man died today,
And although it was someone I don't know,
I'll remember him, even so.

Died today, he died today,
Thousands more died today,
All the lights of life put out,
One thing to remember, their dying shouts.

Died today, he died today,
The man that I knew best,
Now in a silent sleep,
The man that died was me.

Lisa Combellack

DESPERATION

When a time comes and I'm feeling down
I look in the mirror and face a frown.
Some people can't cope with the depression they feel,
Leading to eating disorders or people who steal.
It's strange how different people react, to cope.
Some feel loneliness so rush to elope
Others find a deep black void filling their life,
So abuse their bodies by using a knife
Pain, loneliness, sorrow and guilt
What's needed here is a love to be built.
Love companionship, humour and me,
I'm here to talk to, come and see.

Vicki Terry-Short

GRANDCHILD

My grandad was born in Victoria's reign,
He rode in a pony and trap,
He sat by the range in a high-backed chair,
As I climbed on his lap.

Your grandad, born in the reign of King George,
Has a car, mobile phone and PC,
He's seen Concorde in flight and man on the moon,
And your grandad is me,

Your grandson will come in the reign of which king?
And what will his future world be?
What will he drive in a hundred years time?
And will he look something like me?

Philip Davey

Dedicated to Bella and Flo.

FOUR FAT FEMALE PHEASANTS

Four fat female pheasants were out in a field
On a cold and windy day,
One said to the others, *I really must yield,*
For my feathers keep blowing away.
The eldest stood firm in the teeth of the gale
And said, *Well I never will wilt,*
I've a cousin who stands in the Cairngorms all day,
In a blizzard, not wearing a kilt.

Alan Hayden

Born in Burnham-on-Sea, **Alan Hayden** has interests including reading and painting. "My mother encouraged me to write from an early age. When she died in 1944 I wrote a poem about her which was published in the local paper and I have continued writing ever since," he commented. "My work is influenced by my previous occupations in the police service and farming." Aged 79, Alan is married to Sally and they have three sons and two daughters.

AT THE MINNACK

The full moon shines on the calm dark sea,
Its glittering path lights up the scene
Silhouetting local fishing boats,
Where, with expert ease, men cast their nets.
Beyond stand the high and rugged cliffs
Hiding The Minnack, esteemed by all,
That grass and stone amphitheatre,
The dream-child of great inspiration
Brought into existence by foresight,
Imagination, and persistence,
Now revered and enjoyed by thousands.
Tonight, they arrive, queuing early
To reach favourite seats, bolstered by
Cushions and rugs, soup, pasties and pies,
Sandwiches, cakes, hot drinks and good wine.
The evening's play is too soon over -
All will be remembered and cherished,
The fishing boats, stars and the moon,
The players and that sleepy ride home.
An evening outstanding in time.

Edna S J Williams

THE VISITOR

Today an alien came to my door
Its name, it said, was *I know more*
It spoke with its one eye
Words I could clearly see
I wondered why it was visiting me
It looked a friendly sort of thing
Come inside, I offered, do you like tea?
It came inside with a shuffled hop
Do you like sponge cake, that's all I've got
It refused the cake, it refused the tea
Questions came one after the other
Why do you fight and kill fellow man
Eat animals and fish from a can
I warn you, you've stepped over the line
Your planet is fast on the decline
You poison water and all that you eat
A race like yours I've yet to meet
If I breathe anymore of your air I will surely be dead
Take heed, it warned as it bade me goodbye
I'll never forget that look in its eye as it vanished back up
into the sky

Margaret Beaumont

ZEUS' CAST

Iris of Jasper
Hair akin polished ebony
Allurer of men
Fleece trustee
Sorceress not thee
Alchemy's bride
Scorned from desires artifice
Banished forsaken
O Medea

Jason Dawes

NOVEMBER

Hazy headlights,
Barking dog,
Muffled footsteps
In the fog.
People going,
Don't know where,
Misty ghosts,
Dew in hair.
Eyes that stare,
All are blind,
Following each
One behind.
Human chain,
Barking dog,
Muffled footsteps,
In the fog.

Malcolm Swingler

I WOULD LIKE

I would like to watch a field of corn waving in the breeze,
I would like to lay in an autumn wood on a bed of withered leaves,
I would like to watch the setting sun whilst on a sailing ship,
I would like to feel the cool wind on my face and a salt tang on my lip,
I would like to swim at the foot of a thunderous mountain waterfall,
I would like to watch the receding tide as the sea answers nature's call,
I would like to mount a spirited horse and take a moorland ride,
All these things I would like to do with someone by my side.

Phil Goldman

Born in Manchester, **Phil Goldman** has interests including most sports and walking. "My work is influenced by my inner-self and I am a romantic lover of nature," he pointed out. "I would like to be remembered as a person that has had a very active life in the quest for meeting all challenges." Aged 65, Phil is a swimming coach with an ambition to always be a good example to the young people he works with. He is married to Ann and they have four daughters. "The person I would most like to meet is someone from another planet so we could learn about each other's worlds," added Phil.

LAND OF ETERNAL SERENITY

Far away there is a land
where we can walk in soft warm sand
the water laps upon the shore
where we will live forever more.

The sun shines down on you and me
the sun shines down on the deep blue sea
come take my hand and we can be
loving each other for eternity.

Come let us dip our toes in the sea
let us walk deeper just you and me
take my hand and you take my heart
to this land where we will never part.

I see the sun rise in your eyes
a love that you cannot disguise
I see the moon shine in your heart
a love that will never part.

Gillie Morris

Dedicated to my husband Steve to say thank you for his continuing patience. With love.

GARDEN PARADISE

Relaxing in my garden
On an old deckchair
I see the hand of nature
Transcending everywhere

The beauty of a pale blue sky
Cotton wool clouds drifting by
A breeze that airs a rhapsody
Pleasant buzzing of the bee

Blackbird with his joyous singing
Pretty garden basket swinging
Bedecked with flowers, sheer delight
Colours vivid, rainbow bright

Resting in nostalgic pose
Subtle bouquet of the rose
Fragrant beauty of its bloom
Exquisite in its rare perfume

Pondering to pause and praise
At such marvels in my gaze
With these wonders on display
Tribulations fade away

Frank Beer

NEIGHBOURS ON THE MOVE

Isn't it amazing how friends, from neighbours, grow?
If they hadn't actually bought that house, you would never know.
The sign goes up, you worry, who will actually buy?
Will they be quite so nice? Will they even try?
Then one day the lorry arrives, delivers all their things,
Wardrobes, beds and boxes, all their personal belongings.
One day a casual meeting, later a quick chat or two.
They are so nice in fact, just like the previous ones. Phew.

Susie Burns

CASCADE

Shades of yellow ochre,
Beige and brown,
Jostling, scrambling,
Crumbling, stumbling,
Tumbling down.

Streaming, rushing,
Teeming, crushing,
Falling, sprawling,
Roll to rest,
Till all have come.
The sand is spent,
The time has run,
The eggs are done.

Stella Redman

SIXTY YEARS ON

The lights came on around the land,
The war in Europe was finally done,
Service boys and girls, hand in hand,
Danced in the streets, the battles won.

Sixty years on we celebrated VE Day,
The weather was kind, the sun bright,
Flags flying, the Veterans led the way,
The halt and the lame showed their delight.

All roads closed for the big parade,
Local people on the pavements lined,
Eagerly awaited to see the cavalcade,
The crowds with excitement primed.

The Red Arrows gave a flying display,
Smoke filled sky, red, white and blue
Drifted ever so lazily over the bay,
Aeronautics splendid sight to view,

Well chosen words at the end of day,
At the going down of the sun,
And in the morning,
We shall remember them.

Derrick Roach

TO BE OR NOT TO BE

A poet I request to be,
I love to write and rhyme, you see.

Now, will I share my inner goal?
Depends on who may read my scroll.

A list of names I hold,
A risk of rejection, send it all, be bold.

Now that could be the worst result
That criticism can insult.

Or I'm not loved by all around
and struggle for the smoother ground.

To earn a living being me,
Is satisfaction, totally.

So holding breath I write away
Pouring guts on paper, for display.

Cha Cha Farrow

BAD DAY

I had a bad day today,
The whole world laughed at me,
And yet no-one offered any help,
They stood and stared, pointed and whispered.
I felt so alone
I wished I were a million miles away,
And with a sudden jolt,
I was gone.

Rian Mikalauskas

WAITING

She leaves every morning
And I wait
I don't know where she goes
So I wait

I look through the window
And I wait
To watch and to listen
So I wait

I know that she loves me
And I wait
Her return brings me joy
So I wait

Look, the gate is opening
She is back, she is home
I'll give her my welcome
And she'll give me a bone.

Yvonne Streeter

THE STREET

Stick insects
A stamp collection
A flowering cactus

Sleep walking
Wet beds
And bruises

Surviving the night
Surviving the day
Waiting to see what he uses

Pulled from the bunk bed by
Your hair
Slapped and kicked upon
The chair
Dinner will be ready in
Half an hour
Snow-drops are my
Favourite flower

Sophia Eve Roddan

EVERYDAY HEROES

The house is on fire and you think it's a dream
You wake, choke on smoke, see flames and scream
Is this a nightmare or is this true
Is the hand of death awaiting you?
You begin to crawl on your hands and knees
Praying, *will someone get me out please*

Then just in time strong arms lift you out
Mask over mouth, *breath, love* the firemen shout
Today my life saved, tomorrow it could be yours
Which is why we should all support their cause
To the politicians and leader Mr Blair
It's about time these heroes were treated fair
Can't find the money we hear them say
What rot, I'm just one (alive) reason
they deserve more pay.

Roslyn C Baxter

Dedicated to the memory of my much loved brother John (Shady) Lane, now a hero in some other place. Never forgotten.

Roslyn C Baxter said, "I was born in Plymouth of a naval background, now married with two step-children and one dog. I have written several poems over the years having had a couple published. My first was about Alex Hurricane Higgins in the *Pot Black* magazine. My biggest fantasy would be to have a book published in memory of my late brother and raise huge amounts of money for Leukemia research."

IF LIFE WERE ALL IT WAS MEANT TO BE

If life were all it was meant to be
I would take you by the hand, walk with you
Never let go

If life were all it was meant to be
I would wine and dine you, shower you with flowers
Until the early hours

If life were all it was meant to be
I would kiss your hand and stroke your hair
Caress your cheek, outline your lips with my fingertips

If life were all it were meant to be
I would hold you tight through the night
Kiss you softly, gently caress your innermost soul

If life were all it was meant to be
My love for you I would prove, my soul to you I would give
If you but love me too
I would be yours for as long as I live
If life were all it was meant to be

Lorraine Shaw

A GOOD BOOK

A good book is quite hard to find
You want something you can get lost in
To forget the world you actually live in
To pretend you're elsewhere for a while.
Page after page you just can't put it down
You need to know what happens next
Just one more chapter, you tell yourself
And before you know it, you're done, the end.

Gemma Thomson

PASSING THOUGHTS

When you walk into a garden,
With the scent of every flower
In the cool of any evening
Or after a slight shower.

There you stand alone and silent,
Gaze and goodness knows,
How nature works its wonders,
In the beauty of a rose.

Then slightly bent or leaning,
A snip at your own will.
You handle very tenderly,
To you, is it a thrill?

You very rarely ponder,
Such beauty.
For in this ugly world of ours,
One's shamed by a rose.

Harry Webb

THE BLOOD NURSE

I take a seat and wait my turn and the nerves begin to show
It's only a formality, but for me I just don't know

Each time I go to give some blood it has always been the same
I close my eyes to blot it out, but then there comes the pain

You try it here, you try it there, but again there is rejection
Poor you, I see it in your eyes as you try to reach perfection

It doesn't matter what you do or how many times you try
The veins just won't accommodate and you give an anxious sigh

I want to say to you my dear, my nurse, but more, my friend
That whatsoever you may do we get there in the end

The support that you have given me, for which I am very glad
Gives me the strength to overcome the fears that I have had

Helen Gallagher

PADSTOW BECKONS

Oh lovely Padstow beckons once more.
To the new lifeboat station to adore.
The modern curvy architecture looks good and well
Under today's heavy tidal swell
So when the call comes around
The lifeboat men are seaward bound
Wind, rain, waves are high
Sometimes even under the evening sky
Without these men where would we be,
Many more lives lost at sea.

Michael Woodhouse

SEAGULL

The seagulls soar and kiss the sky
And cry, *I'll be with you as time goes by.*
Think of me on grey morns, skimming cold seas
I'm with you in springtime, I glide on the breeze.
I tantalise tourists at favourite coastal haunts,
I squawk and cry, and peck at you with taunts.
But, just like time, I fly on by,
From dawn to sunset you'll hear my cry.
Through the changing of the seasons,
Year in, year out,
Remember, I live alongside you
When you hear me shout.
Born with the dawning, aging like the sun,
You will remember me, I'm the constant one.
Though I'm captivating, truly I'm free
When you need to spread your wings, think of me.

Sheila Evans

LODDISWELL SHOW

You really must come to Loddiswell Show,
The place where everyone likes to go,
It's always so lovely up at the show,
And everyone says *Oh you really must go.*

There's nowhere else that you can find
A better display of every kind,
There are vegetables and flowers galore,
Cookery goodies and much, much more.

If only I could bake a cake,
Or grow some lovely beans,
Then I could win a lot of cash,
Oh well, only in my dreams.

So please tell your friends to all come along,
So many coming, they can't all be wrong,
Those that don't come will miss such a treat,
And I know there'll be friends there they'll love to meet.

So it's Loddiswell Show,
You can't beat the best,
You'll find nothing better,
In the whole of the west.

Audrey Pope

THE BATH

The body lies motionless, submerged, safe,
Bubbles gently crackle,
Lovingly they cling,
Like a child to the skin,
Knees and breasts protrude like newly formed islands,
All is calm,
The flesh now pink and porous,
Soft as marshmallows on the tongue,
This liquid heaven cannot last,
Time flies, waters chill,
And the cries of the mother's children,
Lay softly in the air.

Tracy Leadbeater

QUESTIONS IN A FLICKERING CANDLE

Are you happy at your work, are you contented with your living?
Is there truth in what you say, is it your best you're giving?

When the sky above is grey and the rain is tumbling down
Is there a sunny smile where you are to be found?

Are you always kind and true, are you loving and forgiving?
Making others happy too, with the joy you are bringing.

Will you accept simplicity, cross out despair forever?
Never be a bore, praising your own endeavour.

Deep desire within us all, every race, creed and colour
Peace, happiness, prosperity will flow, when we learn to love each other.

Patricia Stuckey

A HEART OF STONE

I've fallen in love with a statue, irreparably broken he lies,
Resting far distant from England, unblinking 'neath azure blue skies.
I feel I've known him forever, though he is far older than I.
Through passing of time he has lain there, just waiting for me to pass by.

His body belongs to a temple, part hidden in dusty hot sand,
Unbelievable knowing this sculpture was created by mere human hand.
For aeons of time I have loved him, though of limbs he is sadly bereft,
It's easy to fall for the pharaoh portrayed, from the remnants millennia have left.

I've fallen in love with a statue, battered and broken he lies
It's still unrequited, although I have finally met him with limpid wet eyes.
My time in his presence was sadly too short, but does more than just simply atone,
I know that he can never love me. A king; with a heart made of stone.

Janis Naylor

Dedicated to Ann, I could ask for no better sister in the whole world.

PEVERIL POINT

The enchanting Peveril Point of Dorset,
Where the outstretched beauty lingers on the horizon,
A truly and tranquil day to be awake,
On a perfect late glorious summer's day,
As nature's sky is full of artistry,
Picturesque views of vermillion.

Tiny fishing boats drift across the bay,
With their nets laid and spaced,
And I wondered who is looking up there at the moon's face?
Then, my sleepy head sank low of the deck chair,
And my dreams were of mermaids sitting showy,
On the seashore below.

Sammy Davis

MADONNA

Is this Madonna before me, the girl from my school boy
Days?
The one I watched from a distance when she appeared in
All our plays,
I used to tease her then,
I remember pulling her hair,
But her reaction was to ignore me,
Or transfix me with a stare,
So now I am watching once again this beauty of years ago
This time she appears on the silver screen and she's the
Star of the show,
How lucky I was to have met her and how happy indeed is
My life,
Because she is right here beside me,
This Madonna is my wife.

Betty Aldworth

HOPE

You can share this word with others,
To help it to grow,
Then others who have a bit,
Can grab it when they're low.

Sometimes you need a little,
Sometimes you need a lot,
It's not a big word,
But it can do a lot.

If you use it wisely,
And keep hold of this word,
It can last you a long time,
And any negative thoughts,
Will turn out just fine.

It pops up when you least expect it,
And helps you through the day,
It's never far away,
But if you take someone else's that isn't your own,
It becomes too big to handle,
And leaves you all alone.

Wendy Smith

NO CHIMNEY POT

I'm feeling very worried, and don't know what to do.
Because soon it will be Christmas, and we haven't got a flue.
Santa Claus will soon be here. I don't expect a lot.
But however will he manage without a chimney pot?
We only moved a month ago, I said it wasn't right,
When I looked up and couldn't see a chimney pot in sight.
It's all this central heating, they don't have chimneys anymore,
So do you think when Santa comes, he'll come in by the door?

Margaret Willis

PENNY

The door opened slightly, and a smiling face
Appeared, a dear lady of ninety-four with short grey hair
And glasses, made her way to a comfy armchair,
We chatted about poetry, and drawings and life, we
Found that sunny moments were rife,
A purple plant caught her eyes, and the blue of a
Cloudy summer sky, the morning slipped away so
Fast, like a swan upon a looking glass,
The lasting pleasures of a chat, and knowing the
Beauty of a tortoiseshell cat. The floral display of words
And places, and the memories of other days and
Graces.
A book to share, a story to read, the glimpse of life,
The freedom of a pen. The calling gulls in the misty
Sky, when Portland is ours, and our dreams seem to
Fly.

Susan Emptage

LET'S BE GOOD

Our sense of peace comes from within
When we're entirely free from sin
But who is good and who is strong
To live his life without one wrong?

The fishermen on rivers' banks
Have every reason to give thanks
For days of sunshine with no rain,
But do they think of the fishes' pain?

The athlete on the racing track
For running speed he does not lack,
When proud he's shown clean pair of heels
Does he then think how loser feels?

The husband quarrelling with wife
Because of some domestic strife,
When he's gone out and slammed the door,
Can he his sense of peace restore?

We must be good, we must be strong
And shun what we know to be wrong
For that's the way we'll never cease
To feel that inward sense of peace.

Reg Rowe

IN REPOSE

There are no words to bear the weight of the scene that lies
before me.
The mountains span the cloudless sky, defying all description.

Summer sounds, the fragrant air, nature spreads her
earthly store,
The redbrick of the churches walls is warm, alive, is
breathing.

The mottles stones invite our gaze, the lives relived as we
trace names
We celebrate man's noble deeds and disregard all else.

We sometimes crave eternal rest, resurrection sounds
exhausting
The tantalising question posed, is there more to life than
this?

If you're not aware, you're still informed, granite stones
reposing
Are you watching us with pity? Fear? The silence sounds
like thunder.

Janet Huck

Born in Bournemouth, **Janet Huck** has interests including reading, walking, swimming and the theatre. "I started writing poetry when I was 15 for cathartic reasons," she commented. "My work is influenced by my observations and personal experience and the poets that I admire. I would describe my style as varied." Aged 47, Janet has an ambition to write a poem that will highlight a problem or help others in some way. She is married to David and person she would most like to meet is the playwright Arthur Miller.

THE NIGHTMARE

It was a terrible day at the races
Every horse was a hack
The starter's gate caught in his braces
And he went hurtling up the track
The jockeys had all dismounted
The owners went home in disgust
The punters their losses had counted
And you couldn't see bookies for dust

Albert Lewis

THE MISCHIEVOUS CAT

When my owners are around I'm such a good cat,
I don't steal food or sit on the table, no nothing like that,
I get lots of love, cuddles and praise,
And into her eyes with love I gaze.

But when no one's around it's mischief I seek,
And do all the things that are bad,
I don't know why I do it, for when my owner finds out she'll
be mad.

When I hear her coming I run to meet her with joy,
And she always asks, *Have you been a good boy?*
I shower her with affection then she sees what I've done,
You've clawed the wallpaper and it's clear to see,
Those muddy footprints on the worktops and TV,
I think it's time for me to turn tail and run,
She will soon see I was only having a bit of fun.

Joan Fricker

LADY JAYNE

She goes to bed
With her golden hair
Just right,
Because of the scented bath
She had last night,
She must sleep just right.
Because Lady Jayne sleeps tonight.

David Johnson

MORNING IS BROKEN

Morning is broken, it lies shattered, a thousand crystal shards, never to be remade.
I lay awake and stare at a ceiling as blank as my mind, fleeting thoughts I have to evade.
The warming sun still rises, its tender red caress spilling softly over the lips of the land.
No longer does it warm my skin, feed my body, provide me with the strength to stand.
Fresh is the air, rich in anticipation, hope and the eternal vibrancy of life.
But it lies stagnant in my lungs, burning me, taunting me, cutting like a knife.
The echoes of laughter are gone, no more childish fun masked by dawns playful half-light.
You are now but a severed limb beside me, a ghostly remnant of something so right.
The clouds drift by, no more dragons, no more do we play that lover's game.
Morning will heal, the meaning will return, although it will never ever be the same.

Andrew Gissing

THE FOREST SHEEP

The forest sheep are free to wander where they choose to roam
They flock and roam together in their tranquil forest home
These meek and lovely creatures graze and ramble day by day
They live in peace and harmony with those they meet along the way
With springtime comes the birth of sweet and gentle lambs
Prancing, dancing all around, a happy little band
But alas, the springtime brings dangers unaware
Fine weather drivers come in droves, without a thought or care
They think they own the forest and blast upon their horns
To drive them off the roadside and treat them with such scorn
The meek and gentle creatures think only of their young
Guide them to grazing pastures, soon forget the drivers have come
They teach the young ones road sense, their lives depend upon
To be aware of all the dangers until the cars have gone
Now they look forward to the autumn when trees turn red and gold
The forest settles down for winter and harmony once more unfolds

Eileen Prewett

THE PLEA OF THE DOG

You who have chosen me to own yet would neglect me, look into my eyes,
For they reflect the truth which needs no study,
The dedication that only everlasting loyalty can portray,
And my devotion is steadfast, yes, even unto death.
I am the friend in whom you place your trust,
The patience that is forever, mine is the
Tail that welcomes your homecoming,
The head that doth rest upon your lap to share your solitude.
I am the eyes of your blind,
Your protection for all time,
The friend of all mankind and the gift of your God,
Listen then to my plea, and harm me not.

Vincent Oakes

THE UNSPOKEN WORD

This scourge of the twenty first century,
This *C* of hostility,
That invades our bodies without discrimination,
No consideration for our feelings or others,
An enemy of the immune system,
That we can be forgiven our inhospitality,
That we have a right to fight against
And not be beaten.
Action is the key,
Positivity the force within us,
Medical science advancing daily,
Confrontation the only way,
A network of support to help us,
Cancer need no longer be the unspoken word.

Keith Howard

SOUND OF TOMORROW

See you there - DVD, colour TV, on the show
What's going down?
It's the future now, you know.

Got no time for BBC, ITV over 50 years old
Got no time for e-mail neither
But, it's the future now, you know

Wonder if I'm seeing double, why all this trouble?
Wonder about the sound of tomorrow
Wondering why - it cast a shadow over my life.

Wendy Day

THE CORNER SHOP

Our corner shop has closed now,
The shutters are permanently down.
Empty shelves, no goods on show,
A sad loss for our town.

It was one of those friendly places,
Where customers were greeted by name.
The staff were kind and helpful,
With smiles on their faces.

Deliveries were made to near and far,
Nothing was too much trouble.
Now the doors are closed forever,
So it's goodbye to dear old Spar.

Shirley Clift

THE JOGGERS

Today I met
A pair of happy joggers.
Not a normal sight,
As anyone will say.
They're mostly fat and sighing,
And look as though they're dying,
As they pad and plod along their weary way.

But these two
Had a spring
Like birds upon the wing,
Like children coming out to play.
As they passed me I was yawning
And they both sang out *Good morning,*
And really helped to brighten up my day.

John Anthony

John Anthony said: "I am the other half of a Gemini, who, after a hardworking life, has now put his feet up. This leaves me with the opportunity and the time to wander about, knapsack on my back, observing the world and reflecting upon life's little absurdities. I am hoping to shortly publish a collection of my verses under the title of *Wanderlust.*"

WALKING TO WORK

With red painted shoes, black crust on her heel,
She's slipped into stilts for that summertime feel,
Clock, slip, clack, slip, click and Pantene Pro-V,
And that shiny new hair flick as she overtakes me,
While weightwatchers samba round lycra tight glutes,
Gay and straight clamber to touch up her roots,
High fashion, low belt-line, Max Factored for all weathers,
She's resprayed her sunshine and brazilianned her nethers,

White sling backs on kilter, she's ready and able,
To highlight her assets and the Shoe Fayer price label.

And as I watch the sway of her figure,
My beer belly drops and bald patch grows bigger,
My left shoulder aches for her thimble sized bag,
And I move one step closer to being just like my dad.

Glenn Mower

MARRIAGE VIEWS

My wife's called Susie
She's young and boozy,
Sits all day in the jacuzzi,
Some say she's a floozy,
But at ninety, one can't be choosy.

My husband is long in the tooth,
Perhaps our age difference is uncouth,
Some think I've sold my youth,
But money makes you weatherproof,
Well, that's the truth.

Stella Lamb

DRACULA

His eyes are beautiful, they own your soul
Your body moves you have no control
He rubs your arm and leaves you tingling and burning
Your heart is thumping, your insides churning
He grins an evil smile, his teeth pointed and sharp
You feel afraid yet sleep to the sound of the harp
The pain is quick and sharp.
You feel your life being drawn out of yourself
The thing draws away its mouth fresh with blood
You sink down to the floor with a thud
He walks away, you know you must resist it
But he plays with you like a cat, calling you as he leaves,
flying like a bat.

Maryrose Ferrier

THE GYPSIES

I saw them on the open road
The caravan, the heavy load,
The skewbald horse with measured pace
That takes them on from place to place,
They have no wealth or blessed abode
Save the crying wind and lonesome road.

Raymond Pearce

THE OWL

There is a large owl that lives in a barn behind the back of my house.
You never see him by day, he is as quiet as a mouse.
Late at night he emerges to hunt, with his talons as sharp as knives,
He is looking for his supper, the little rabbits had better run for their lives.
The owl is gliding over a field, his eyes are fixed on his prey,
Sweeping down he makes his kill, the rabbit could not get away.
His talons struck sinking into the body and held on very tight,
Then he took the meal back to the barn in the dark of the night.
Later a very satisfied owl flies and sits on my fence to screech,
For the rest of the night he carries on and keeps me from my sleep.

Judy Robinson

FATHER'S DAY

It's Father's Day.
That's when we say we 'preciate our dads.
For all the mechanical advice, and the loans we've had.
So here he is, I present our Chris, or Bamps as many know him.
Our president, or captain, the subject of this poem.
In that fine head, we find a mind, keen and sharp and quick.
On Sudoku, crosswords, or maths, he is still slick.
And now he sails on journeys long, his new boat bigger, and shiny.
His crew obey every command, when rounding Cowes on the briny.
So here's to dad, or Bamps, or Chris. The man who carries and cooks.
A decent chap, and my old pap, *The source of my good looks.*

Giles Highnam

Born in Salisbury, **Giles Highnam** has interests including disabled sports, reading and fishing. "My work is influenced by my family, friends and life," Giles explained. "I would describe my style as verging on the comic and I would like to be remembered as a survivor who made a difference." Aged 38, Giles is an administrator with an ambition to learn to fly. "The person I would most like to meet is Margaret Thatcher as I believe she shaped my young life."

SILENCE

Silence is when you can hear things.
Listen,
The burning sun waking to shine over the pretty earth,
The steamy frost covering a busy world,
The pure snow pittering and pattering as it lands,
Or the gentle wind whispering in everyone's ear.

Charlotte Edmonds

CHARLIE

Get up, get up, you sleepy head,
It's really time you left your bed.
Exercise is what you need,
Before you have another feed.

Sammy came up looking for you,
He's already had a mouse or two.
That was his breakfast, what he likes best,
Off he's gone home now, for a nice long rest.

If we had your life, with no worries at all,
Just to sleep and play, and sit on the wall.
Your bed and board, two meals a day,
With nothing to do but sleep and play.

You had nowhere to live, so we took you home,
Our most beloved tabby cat, no more to roam.
With us you have settled, now happy and content,
So thank you dear Charlie, for us you were meant.

Gillian Layzell

GRANNY'S WALKING STICKS

My Granny had two walking sticks
She kept beside the bed
If I wouldn't go to sleep
She would poke me on the head.
The walking sticks had badges
Of gold, silver and red
They reminded her of her travels
She turned to me and said.
She will want a badge of the *Pearly Gates*
When she goes up to Heaven
And someone to nail it upon the stick
Near the badge from *sunny Devon.*
The years rolled by for Granny
And she soon became quite weak
She still kept her sticks beside the bed
And didn't even speak.
Now my dear Granny passed away
I turned to my mother and said
How will Granny walk in Heaven
When her sticks are by the bed?

Violetta Ferguson

MEMORIES

Upon the wings of butterflies
And lonely summer breezes rest
Memories, such memories,
Of one such face that nature kissed.

Upon white freedom's gaping wings
And Father Time's mind of mist
Lie memories, such memories
Of one such face that I shall miss.

Melanie Jones

I'LL ALWAYS LOVE YOU

I'll always love you, all my life
From the moment I saw you, till you became my wife
You were the one with kind loving ways
I'll always love you for the rest of my days

We've travelled together on this long winding road
But we helped each other carry the load
For I could not have done it on this journey through life
Without you by my side as my loving wife

We had some good times, we had some bad times
We had some happy times, we had some sad times
I would not change this life I've had
We had more good times than we had bad

I was so lucky the day I met you
When all my dreams had come true
You were the one with kind, loving ways
I'll always love you for the rest of my days

Maurice Carpenter

THE CHRISTIAN AID COLLECTOR

Going around the houses, I must have heard it all,
The wife deals with that stuff, and *I haven't got the thingy.*

But one husband ran up to me saying,
Here you are, we're going out now, so take it while you can.

These men of merry Fishponds, God bless them all.
You did better than the housewives, because you were on the ball.

But the best house was the last one, with a cheery
How are you? And, *come on in and see us*, from Diana and Anthony.

They gave some change, so somewhere a child won't have to walk six miles for water,
The kindness in them shone.

They gave me the best of all gifts,
The gift of a cup of tea, and friendship.

God bless you all.

Caroline Vennard

SOUNDS

Dinner's ready, Jenny dear,
That's a sound I like to hear,
There are other sounds I listen for,
Like the knock of the postman on the door.

The sound of the lark on a clear day,
The clap of thunder when skies are grey,
The patter of rain when I'm lying in bed,
The jingle of coins when I've been in the red.

The sound of music when I'm alone,
When the call is for me if I hear the phone,
The shout of goal when I watch the game,
The crackle of fire on the bonfire flame.

Best the school bell at a quarter to four,
Then I'm off to other sounds I adore.

Pamela J Hacking

Born in Plymouth, **Pamela J Hacking** has interests including reading, walking and jigsaws. "I started writing poetry a few years ago and find that I am inspired by events in life," she pointed out. "I would describe my style as impulsive and I would like to be remembered kindly." Aged 77, Pamela is retired and the person she would most like to meet is the politician Tony Benn. "He was always so genuine and I have always admired him," explained Pamela, who has written over 30 poems but not had any published until now.

YOU

Whenever you are near
All doubts absolutely disappear
You keep me calm
And I know I will always be free from harm
Just knowing you are close
Keeps my mind totally clear
Your continual support
Means you are never far from my thoughts
I'm reassured when our hands touch
For me, at least, it means so much

Nicola Woodley

HEAVENLY SNIPPETS

Sitting up late, chatting to the best friend of my life,
Fortunately enough that friend is also my wife,
We talk and drink, thrashing out problems we have to face,
Wondering how to put teenage boys in their place.

Sitting at boundary's edge, watching tussle with bat and ball,
Cricket, most refined sport of all.

Feet up in the garden, listening to the grass grow,
Such an air of serenity, just go with the flow,
Watch those birds, are they rooks or be they crows?
They all know, but none of them shows.

What should we think of when things are rough and tough?
Life's ingredients need some leaven?
Just to contemplate the above, that's quite enough,
So we'll all see some snippets of heaven.

Michael Elliott

JUST A CHILD

What is this vision before me,
With a mind and a will of its own,
A mind to think and a will to be wild,
But basically knowing it is just a child.

A child can be loving, a child will be good,
A child will follow as children should,
A child can be friendly, a child can be kind,
A child inherits what we leave behind.

This vision before me will daily grow,
Unless it is cared for, its knowledge is low,
Examples are copied and carefully filed,
And watching us daily is the same little child.

A child has a temper, a child gets fraught,
A child is naughty and has to be taught,
A child can be laughing or a child can cry,
This child needs help from you and I.

This vision before me needs loving care,
A trusting hand, and hope to share,
For this special person may we all be made mild,
Tomorrow's adult, remember, is still just a child.

Margaret Cawsey

REJOICE

Let us rejoice in the wakening
Of nature all around,
Leaves and flowers bursting forth
From the cold and barren ground.

Let us rejoice in the beauty,
The freshness, the hope, and the joy,
Let us rejoice for it's Easter,
With a message the world cannot destroy.

New life and faith it brings to all,
That's the promise Easter imparts,
Reminding of hope for the future,
A message that lifts up the heart.

Death and hell were defeated
On that first Easter morn,
Bondage was turned to freedom,
The fetters from Satan were torn.

Now Heaven's gates are open,
To all who take Jesus as King,
Rejoice and be glad for it's Easter,
Let our praise to Heaven ring.

Florence L Brain

Born in Letchworth, **Florence L Brain** has interests including gardening. "I started writing poetry after my retirement and my work is influenced by my faith," she explained. "I would describe my style as plain but with a message and I would like to be remembered as a faithful warrior of the Salvation Army." Aged 88, Florence is a Salvation Army officer and a former nurse. She is married to Derrick and has written sermons and many poems.

I WISH

I wish that all the cars would simply go away,
Back to peace and quiet, and life a leisurely way.
A country cottage garden with trellis around the door,
The heady scent of roses you can smell and so adore.
Borders full of colour, lupins standing tall,
Buzzing bees and butterflies, dragonflies dip and fall.
Tree-lined lanes and hedgerows, the smell of new mown hay,
The clip clop of a horse and cart, going on its way.
I know it's wishful thinking, things will never be the same,
But I have many memories of that cottage down the lane.

Joan Lake

TREASURED SIMPLICITY

Make the most of what you have, it won't last forever,
Those moments of content, you just need to treasure.
Like riding a bike for the very first time,
Or watching the birds fly high in the sky.
It won't always be hard, no need to be clever,
The earth is your eyes, you're stronger together.
As the wind whispers through the spring green trees,
We can't help but listen, we fall to our knees.
Admire what's around you, even if it isn't real,
Be grateful you can see the light, be grateful you can feel.
Make sure to see the sunrise, make sure to see the stars,
Make sure you hold your head high, but don't forget your scars.

Sam Davis

ABORTION

Things have changed since that day
When I decided to do away
With what I had growing inside,
That one thing I could not hide.

What a mess I've made of life
Since that day the real me died,
Things can never be the same,
The pain inside will never fade.

The baby that I gave away,
So I could live my life this way,
And do the things I wish to do,
And see the people that I choose.

Though so selfish it may sound,
But there are things that I found
That would turn my life around

And change me into someone new
Which would eventually see me through
And lead me here to meet you,

Here at last, the ghosts can lay,
And the pain can fade away.

Lynsey Wootton

DAYDREAM

I have a fantasy, running through my brain
Of a millionaires lifestyle, I know it's insane
To think of sleek boats, and rolling blue seas
Golden sands lined with waving palm trees
To travel the world in a streamlined yacht
Visit tropical islands and small lush eyots
With blue lagoons and magical grottos
The smell of exotic plants pervading my nose
Brilliant coloured butterflies dancing in the breeze
The shrill call of parrots, and the humming of the bees
Under the heat of the sun, with skies so blue
I wish my fantasy could come true
But with a deep sigh, I must get on
To get my housework and washing done

Patricia Shellis

GOODBYE

Why do people leave us?
The question drives you nuts,
Each time it gets harder,
As the curtain shuts.

I have loved and lost,
From very young until today,
Apparently time makes it easier,
So they say.

When all is quiet and peaceful,
I lie and think of you,
I know one day we'll meet again
And that's what gets me through.

Jacqui Shipway

ENGLAND

England's countryside,
Peaceful and green,
An English rose,
Best ever seen.

England's meadows,
Taste of spring,
English Sundays,
Church bells will ring.

England's mountains,
Rivers and lakes,
The English oak,
Let's never forsake.

Douglas Hoyle

Born in Bristol, **Douglas Hoyle** has interests including writing and the church. "I started writing poetry about 11 years ago when my wife died," he remarked. "My work is influenced by my religious beliefs and I would like to be remembered as a good husband, father and grandfather." Aged 74, Douglas is a retired printer. He is the widower of Shirley and has children Wayne and Richard. "The person I would most like to meet is the actress Dame Helen Mirren because I would like to talk to her about portrayal of my number one lady, the Queen," added Douglas.

JUST ME

I am a breeze you can not see,
or a cloud far out at sea.

I am an idea, a pause, or just a thought,
the values that I was taught.

I am a whisper, or just a hint,
a rush or a sudden sprint.

I am that which is only just there,
or a soul that is laid bare.

I am the past, now gone,
or words not yet written for a song.

I am the meaning for what is to be,
of the future, what can I see?

I am as I was and will be,
all that I am, is only just me.

Colin Threader

PUBITE ALRIGHT!

To the pubite I met the other night
Because everything I said was wrong
But what he said was right

I think I need the practice
To make what's said my right
So I should spend more hours down the pub each night

Practice they say makes perfect
I've tried with all my might
But until I become a pubite
I'll leave it to him *alright!*

Maurice W Fawcett

THOMAS

Nine years in the Army,
Blanks spite and shine,
Four minutes to get in line,
Small pack, knapsack, kitbag rifle,
Sergeant shouting at merest trifle,
Pick up that bloody rifle.

Wading through paddy fields,
Sleeping in holes,
Passing bloody bodies of departed souls,
Crawling out for *stand to* in freezing mist,
Why the hell did I ever enlist?
But the camaraderie was something
Not to be missed.

Bee K Watson

THE HAPPIEST DAYS OF YOUR LIFE

Lucky you, you bloomin' kids,
I'd say much worse, but you're only kids.
Don't do that, stop picking your nose.
I saw that. I'm everywhere.
Because I'm an adult and I don't care.
The big difference
Between young and old,
From being a child to becoming an adult,
Adults just crash the cars, shoot the guns,
Start the wars, chop the trees, spill the oil,
Drink the booze, smoking too,
Some really naughty ones take drugs.
Spoiling the world, just for you.
What we do, you'll do too.

Alex Date

Born in Reading, **Alex Date** has interests including reading, films and sports. "I started writing poetry as a teenager to escape the limitations of reality," he commented. "My work is influenced by tragedy, hypocrisy, outrage, irony and beauty and I would describe my style as cynical and bitter."

SNOWDROP

Like a graceful ballerina,
She stands in gown of white,
Upon the frozen clods of earth,
Fluttering in the light.

She comes to us when all seems dead,
Shoots forth her leaves of green,
Dons her pretty dancing dress,
To grace our garden scene.

What fragile beauty snowdrop wears,
So weak and yet so strong,
She trembles there in icy winds,
And says *spring won't be long.*

Pam Jewell

SPOTS

Spots are strange, spots are weird
Overnight they just appear
They follow no path, follow no route
They just stand out in your birthday suite

Colin Mann

NO VASES PLEASE

How the breeze sways their heads
Of vibrant yellows, blues and dazzling reds,
The stems they dance, to bring romance
To any that their eyes would glance.

Bright colours are their pleasure ways,
Inviting lacy, fragile mites,
The food of nectar in their cups,
That soaks the sun and moisture up.

'Tis such a shame, when flowers cut,
To stand on table all bunched up,
Confined to vase, or some such thing,
Restricted life, seems such a sin.

Denied life's cycle of events,
Seems such a moral offence,
Intrinsic earth, do you not lament?
For all the nurtured time you've spent.

Betty Bywater

MY LOVE TO YOU

My love for you will never die,
There's plenty in my heart,
I've kept it there, just for you,
It's been there from the start.

It started like a rose bud,
And now it's in full bloom,
It grew and grew from morn 'til night,
It's only just for you.

Love is a thing that's come to stay,
That's if it is true love,
It means so much to both of us,
As precious as a dove.

So when we have our ups and downs
And can not both agree,
We must sit down and find a way,
There is one you will see.

So treasure it all you can,
It may not last for long
And if you love me as I loved you,
I'm sure it can't go wrong.

Joan Rowland

SPORTS

In rain and snow, fog and sun,
With shaped leather, how they run.
Money placed upon the race,
Four legs set a fevered pace.
Metal, rubber, very fast,
Round the circuit going past.
Wood on water, strain the oar,
Not much change since days of yore.
People wearing funny shoes,
Taking part for sponsors' dues.
Many sports in many ways,
Mine is dreaming, nowadays.

Percy J Harrison

A BIRTHDAY TO REMEMBER

The party dress I chose to wear was taffeta and lace
I felt a million dollars, what a shame about my face
I'd sat too near the open fire to dry my flaxen curls
So now my face was ruby red and marked with ugly whorls
I soon forgot my facial plight when friends came through the door
But everyone was so surprised to see my face so raw
I tried to change the subject and turned the lights down low
Perhaps some music would detract and help me hide my woe
Before we know, the table's set, at last it's time to eat
I shan't forget that birthday bash and now avoid the heat.

Barbara M Crisp

FIVE BONE WANDS

A clock rips through its ticks as surely as sight blinds
true memory.
Here, with distant will, another lisping distort binds
Five bone wands to five bone wands.

Steady patter tracks the blinking scraps uphill, my friend,
and over the otherside,
Five bone wands still grip five bone wands.
Their magnet whole, magic thought attracts steel, though
still souls retract,
And five bonds through five
Trace their blood-lines back to bone-birthing earth.
A pattern followed by the grip of
Five bone wands on five bone wands.
An infant's grip. Life's first cry to, the last groan of
a sinking ship.
Crossed palms quiver but stick,
Ever-glue knits chips of each to the other
And those five fragile twigs,
Five grasping organs,
Five mark-makers,
Grip as finely as time to itself.

Wooden lids bang down a final tick
Which rips the clock from its hinges.
But five bone wands still grip five bone wands.

Patrick Jefferies

THE DEMON INSIDE

Fingers in the till buying gear for your ills.
I go out walking in the middle of the night,
I was confronted by a man with danger in his eyes
Come with me he whispers in the cold,
His pale gaunt face sends shivers through my bones.

He wants me as his apprentice for a life fuelled by crime,
Will I go, won't I? He's waiting to be told,
It's a one off offer he explains, *if I may be so bold.*
I look at him intensely and come on in from the cold.

Marc Richards

FIFTY EIGHT

How did I get to be this age
Without going round the bend,
All I hear is, where's this, where's that
Will it never end.
Have you seen my homework,
Did you move my book,
Where's my trendy jacket,
Who put it on that hook.

Being a granny, nothing's changed
Where's my sponsor form you had,
Where have you put my trousers,
Did you mend the zip for me,
Cool, they don't look bad.

At least the washing pile has shrunk,
There's more room on the line,
But will I still be slightly sane,
When I'm fifty nine.

Margaret R Punter

DAISY

Precious child of my child
A treasure sent from above
Sweet, gentle and innocent baby
Welcomed with so much love

Millennium child you are special
In oh so many ways
A smiling, knowing bundle
The answer to all my prayers

Be sure, I'll watch you grow proudly
And find interest in all that you say
Even your smallest achievements
Will be acclaimed along the way

I searched for a gift to bring you
That would last your whole life through
Something that would be the measure
Of how I felt about you

Nothing I found was worthy
To match the gift from above
The most precious gift I can offer
Is my unconditional love

Angela James

Dedicated to Daisy Elizabeth Hill, my first grandchild, born in September 2000. Her sweetness and my joy were inspirational.

THE WORLD

The world is turning much too fast
This high technology is here to last
So much is yet for scientists to find
Will they ever have peace of mind
Working hard for a solution
To rid this world of its pollution.
Are we mere mortals ready to confess
That we are to blame for this dreadful mess
Can we help in any way
To keep this contamination at bay?
Or will we just lay back and say
We will think about it some other day

Valerie Hembry

THE INVALID

Laying flat upon your back
Vaguely like a potato in a sack.
Wondering what on earth to do
Looking to the trip to the loo
As daily exercise and different view.

The wooden board on which I sleep
Gives great relief to pain down deep.
Sciatica isn't much fun,
When you would rather get up and run.
But family and friends are just great
Which I very much appreciate.

Helen Guymer

TOYS OF YESTERDAY

Spinning tops, rocking horse
Guiders made by hand.
Rubber wheels, spikey spokes
Stolen from a pram.

Marbles round and glassy,
Bulls-eyes big and brown
Torn jeans and dirty hands
Playing on the ground.

A fort for all your soldiers
Made from a cardboard box,
Cowboy hats, skipping ropes
To tie yourself in knots.

Dolls houses, sweetie shops
Airfix, models, and glue.
Those were toys of yesterday
Toys that we once knew.

Patrick Hutchinson

TEN YEARS OF DETECTION

D is for daughter
Dorothy's darling daughter
D is for dedication
Yours to the nation
D is for daring
This you will know
D is for devotion
You have more than a notion
D is for destiny
Hopelessly, happily
That you will be effective
With a D for detective

Dorothy S Keene

ENTRANCED

Oh, golden globe,
Far out to sea,
You seem to beckon,
Call out to me,
You light a path,
For me to follow,
Your voice is warm,
Not cold or hollow,
Though sorely tempted,
I must decline,
But wait once more
For you to shine.

The clouds moved by,
The wave crests danced,
But I couldn't leave,
For I was entranced.

Clive Blake

THE MEANING OF TRUE BLISS

This evening's sun setting slowly across the beach,
Our kids running around in the pink water's edge.
You, my partner, my friend, my lover, hand over a peach,
For you my undying love I do pledge.
Memories of the woodland walks that we have done,
Picnics on the moors, days out with the dogs.
Countless hours of endless fun,
The bonfires roasting marshmallows sat on a log.
To you I owe so much, you really are the best,
Before we got together is one big fog.
Snuggled on the sofa at night, both glad of the rest.
For you I want the world.
For me a big hug and a sweet kiss.
Our son and daughter I have twirled.
For you have shown me the meaning of true bliss,
Within your arms I now lay curled.

Paul Fancett, Crediton, Devon

Dedicated to Anya for loving me and letting me be a dad twice to Alice and Callum. I love you all.

Born in Tiverton, **Paul Fancett** has interests including reading, writing and fishing. "When I was 18 I started living on my own and this inspired to think a lot more and to begin writing," he explained. "I would like to be remembered as someone who always tried to improve himself and was always truthful." Aged 33, Paul works as a welder and fabricator and has ambitions to own his own house and business and see those around him live in happiness. He and his partner Anya have children Callum and Alice. "The people I would most like to be for the day are my children to see if I am a good father to them," added Paul.

PARTIES?

I haven't had too many parties, as I was told:
probably money reasons, *parties, you're getting too old!*
Most of the time, I was in hospitals or at Treloars.
Oh! I wish I had several more!

The last one was my 40th, by my ex-wife,
apart from Hannah, this was my 3rd. High-life!
Also, not neighbours or family, only been invited to by
three.
Vicky H-W, a female biker, and Sally C.

This year has changed.
Gillian is giving me a 50th birthday party
so I hope a lot will come, like work's sexy Indian *babe,* Arti.
So, what is a party? I never really know.
Drinking, sex, *oh I wish!*, talking, I better follow the flow!

Civil Service Club is booked, so is the DJ,
I hope everyone loves the buffet!
Shame Janet can't come, but is down with the flu,
so Gillian, my sister, may I say a big thank you!

Barry Ryan, Winchester, Hampshire

Born in Winchester, **Barry Ryan** has interests including cinema, television and ten-pin bowling. "I am disabled and I started writing poetry in hospital," explained Barry. "I would describe my style as personal and I like to write about subjects which are of a deep, personal importance to me." Aged 50, Barry would like to be remembered as a nice, caring and honest person and has ambitions to become famous. "I would love to talk to other poets and they can email me on poetbarry57@aol.com," added Barry.

A LOCAL POEM COULD WIN YOU £1,000

A poem about someone or something in your home town could win you £1,000 in a free poetry competition.

All you have to do is write a poem about something or someone from your home town, or even write a poem about your home town. £1,000 goes to the winner of the competition which closes on 31st December.

The competition is open to poets of all ages and is designed to encourage new poets to get more involved in writing poetry.

"Poetry is one of the most accessible art forms and more people should be writing poems. Many new poets are unearthed by competitions like this," said Peter Quinn, Managing Director of United Press which is running the competition.

You can post up to 3 entries for the competition. They must all have a maximum of 160 words and 20 lines each. You can find out more about last year's winner by visiting the website www.unitedpress.co.uk and also find out more about this competition and how to enter by email.

You can post your entries (with a LOOSE stamp if you want to be sure of a reply after the competition has closed) to United Press, Admail 3735, London, EC1B 1JB.

The 2007 winner was Marjorie Beachill of Wath upon Dearne, South Yorkshire who has featured in the media including local and national press.

The 2006 winner was a poem all about his home town - Billinge - Lancashire - by Owen Lowery who has since been featured in the media and has given poetry readings. Owen has since been selected by United Press to be an editor on its webzine, Voice.

Full Colour

Stephen King, Mark Twain, Lord Byron, George Bernard Shaw, Beatrix Potter, Jane Austen, Rudyard Kipling and Edgar Allen Poe were just a few of the writers who began their careers by contributing to their publication costs. So, if you decide to produce your own book, you are in elevated company.

Thanks to new technology you can now even print your own poetry book with a full colour cover, starting at just £267. (Or only £168 in black and white onto marble card).

You can select your colour cover from a wide range of dazzling images which can be viewed by visiting our website at *www.unitedpress.co.uk*. If you don't have a computer you can go to your local library or internet cafe to see the images.

When you go onto the website click on *publications* then click on *book covers*. This will allow you to view all the many covers which you can choose from. Or you can provide your own photo or painting.

United Press produces everything from books of poetry to novels in a variety of covers including softback and hardback. Just telephone 0870 240 6190 and we will put details and a free sample in the post to you straight away.

For all writers, getting into print is the pinnacle of ambition. Thanks to United Press you now have that ambition easily within your reach.

❑ *You can also visit our website to find out about the charity work done by United Press.*